ENTREPRENEURIAL
MINISTRY

The Catalyst to Community Social Change

Judy Benjamin Henderson

 www.trafford.com

North America & international
toll-free: 1 888 232 4444 (USA & Canada)
fax: 812 355 4082

CONTENTS

DEDICATION

In loving memory of my father, Earnest Benjamin (1918-2009), who made it possible for me to encounter, understand, and become tutored by the first entrepreneur servant of faith known to me—himself—and who taught me by his living example that the purpose of my life is far greater than my own personal fulfillment, peace, or even my happiness. However, he explained that in time, I would discover my identity and purpose through a closer relationship with Jesus Christ. I am grateful for his wisdom.

ACKNOWLEDGEMENTS

Every accomplishment in life is the result of the contribution of many individuals who, both directly and indirectly, share their gifts, talents, and wisdom with us. My incredibly gifted staff at Empowerment Resource Associates Inc. and the RIGHT Foundation are essentially the laboring power behind the ministry. Without them, I could not be away from the office pioneering, much less take the time to write this book. I thank God for sending me staff who are individually creative, whose egos are not bigger than their hearts, who are not too proud to be humble nor too timid to stand up for what is right, and who serve at-risk communities unselfishly.

I am most grateful to my husband, Bob, for his love, confidence, and continuous support of me over the many years of marriage. My inspiring children, Robert Junior and Yolanda, who are faithful and competent executive board members of Empowerment. I am most grateful to my mother, Rose Nell, who nurtured and motivated me to become my best self; my sister Eva L. Slater, who often used her deaconess heart and spiritual discernment during late hours of the night to understand my purpose and further acknowledged the call on my life through promotion; and the rest of my siblings, who allowed me to learn these truths about life along my journey. My friend Stella White, who stuck by me and believed in the importance of living on purpose no matter what the cost. Sike Mbette and Charles Mouteng of African Christian

Fellowship, who served as mentors and Bible study partners along the way.

Without you folks in my life, my writing task would have been sorely hampered. I thank you and love you for your gentle spirits and kindness of heart.

INTRODUCTION

> Of life's two chief prizes, beauty and truth, I found the first in a loving heart and the second in a laborer's hand.
>
> Khalil Gibran

In awe of how God has used me by molding my daily vocation into a ministry that spiritually empowers and brings emotional healing and hope to constituents, I am humbly committed to promoting community entrepreneurial ministry. It is my belief that God purposely places each of us where we are geographically and relationally to perform the tasks that were created for our predestined service. His desire is for us to be salt and light in the world. Our work in these communities provides the privilege of introducing life-changing, Godly principles to those who live in our flawed society and desperately need our help through service.

This book will provide a capsulated view of how God used me in my vocation and gift of leadership to bring empowering resources to numerous people through a staff of creative, individualized, like minds that work in the ministries as therapeutic and spiritual counselors. I will share the process of my transformational thinking, which ultimately developed my world view, which further seeks biblical integrity and spiritual faithfulness for its success. Other chapters will expose the spiritual gifts and vocational skills of preaching ministers whose work has stood the test of time. Their spiritual, political, social, and economic advocacy has produced social change that has global significance and presence.

Our forebearers saw this country as a land set aside by God as a place of refuge and hope for believers who would conform their lives to religious principles of conduct. For most of human history, no one ever had to search for the sacred. Every culture's core practiced some type of cult or ritual. Religion was the womb of civilization (Woodword 1994). For most of our history, religion was the core force that created our sense of morality. Religion defined good and evil and provided the context for human interactivity.

Over the years, we have lost our religious moral roots. Since work is the place where we spend most of our time, some of us tend to look for the sacred from our work. However, our work has lost meaning. The frustration and anxiety we feel relates to our value and focus on the material and the absence of spirit. The workplace is not only an economic site but a prime locus of life itself. Therefore, it is evident that people in all kinds of occupations are raising their voices for a spiritual foundation in order to coexist in a world full of chaos. The feeling of closeness and oneness has lost its relevance and is no longer evident in societies.

Research by Jacobson (1994) strongly suggests that experienced leaders and other members in our work organizations are redefining work to include satisfaction of deep inner needs for spiritual identity and spiritual satisfaction. This spiritual identity among the ministers and leaders must be evident in the work as it is being done in our communities. The presence of the spirit of God will ultimately set the tone for community social change.

While many of our communities are spiraling down to total destruction, I am ever aware that they need to be visited by the Lord for sustenance.

We need to take hold of these communities and claim the ever-constant word of God as their balm in Gilead. As the Word said:

If my people, who are called by my name, shall humble themselves and pray, and seek my face, and turn from their wicked ways, then I will hear from heaven and will forgive their sin, and will heal their land. (2 Chronicles 7:14)

Many entrepreneurial servants are called by God to labor in the secular field and plant seeds of reconciliation, hope, and love to the un-churched, lost, and unloved. For many in the community, this will be their only chance to experience Christ. These servant providers are not local or foreign missionaries but rather businessmen and businesswomen, respectfully known as entrepreneurs. Their vision of this service and desire to give birth to it was first conceived in their spirit. The spiritual revelation manifested itself to them as a calling to ministry or, in other words, their God-given purpose for soul winning. As a direct result of following their purpose, they became change agents for humanity.

The entrepreneurial ministry is an extension of the traditional church. It promotes and encourages community outreach ministry at its best. The following chapters will help these servants to recognize, celebrate, and accept their call to ministry. A better understanding of this unique ministry will influence them to embrace their laboring role in the body of Christ, which further advances the kingdom of God through reconciliation, healing, hope, and love for such a time as this.

CHAPTER 1

THE JOURNEY IS THE DESTINATION

> *In the hero stories, the call to go on a journey takes the form of a loss, an error, a wound, an unexplainable longing, or a sense of a mission. When any of these happens to us, we are being summoned to make a transition. It will always mean leaving something behind, . . . The paradox here is that loss is a path to gain.*
>
> *David Richo*

My Personal Testimony

Having fun in the big city would explain the way I rebelled in college to the way I had been brought up. You see, my parents decided for me that I would follow their example and become an 'outgoing Christian' like they were. At the age of 12, they lured me to this old-fashioned two-week revival service so that I could 'seek the Lord', as they called it. I did listen to all that was said each night; however, it was not until the final night of services that I responded as they had hoped, by giving my life to Jesus.

I really needed to be sure about this matter of salvation. So my prayer on the night of my acceptance was, 'Lord, after I give my life to you, would you respond to me in a way that I know, that I know, that I know, you heard and received my prayer.' After which, I waited on my knees, and there seemed to have been no response. I continued to trust, and a couple of minutes later, the power of God came upon me, and I felt as light as a feather as I gracefully walked around the church, confessing to numerous people that I had found Jesus and he was in my heart. What a freeing and joyful experience that was. On my ride home with my parents, I could finally relax from the days of exhaustion that stemmed from my anticipation of finding the Lord. I learned from that experience that seeking and finding Christ was not as difficult as I had thought. However, I found out that Jesus was a gift given to me. It is free! I was free from the pressure of fulfilling my parents' expectations, and I had a new peace. For Jesus said in 1 Peter 5:7, 'Cast all your anxiety on Him because He cares for you.'

When the time came for me to be out from under my parents' leadership, I decided to try living my own way and experiencing new things. Soon after junior college, I got married, had two children, and had the beginning of a budding career. I had many accomplishments in the following years, but felt that they were due to my own abilities, and I prayed less and received less relationship from the Lord. I eventually squeezed him out. Furthermore, no matter what I did, what I bought, or what I received, I found no fulfillment. I could be in a room full of people and still feel as if I was the only one there. I longed to fill this empty space in my heart.

One night about twenty years ago, I was making tidy our rarely used third-floor guest room and found a copy of a devotional book by Marilyn Hickey, which lay next to the Bible. I did not buy this book, but it appeared interesting. I thought that maybe one of our visiting family members might have left it. I started to read it and look up passages from the Bible. I came across 1 Corinthians 3:16, which says, 'Know ye not that ye are the temple of God, and that the Spirit of God dwells in you.' This scripture relit a spark in me that felt good. I continued to read, and Marilyn Hickey was sharing experiences very similar to mine, and that was when I really understood that the Word of God was the key. This reading went on for months. It was during this time that I developed a closer relationship with God and found meaning in life by discovering my purpose. This purpose gave me hope, and my life started to make sense. I then realized how blessed and privileged I was to live in an age that produced world-renowned leaders who were effectual in outreach ministries. I found substance in my life and a foundation on which I based decisions, allocated my time, and used the resources open to me. I realized that I wanted Him to use my life. To make a long story short, He has! God has placed me in a ministry to uplift the depressed and downtrodden, the people that society has ostracized. Ministry services are offered at my nonprofit agency, the Resource Initiatives Giving Hope through Training (RIGHT) Foundation, and later Empowerment Resource Associates Inc., a behavioral health and wellness organization. My career is now fulfilling and is one of service to others in need. The pay is low, but the rewards are high. I now have the joy of following in the footsteps of Jesus. My prayer is that one day all of the ones that I provide and influence in service provision will come to know and follow Christ and worship him in spirit and in truth.

The Journey

As stated by A. W. Tozer, 'It is not what a man does that determines whether his work is sacred or secular, it is why he does it.'

It was in 1993 that I started on a more mature spiritual journey in service to others based on living out my faith. The key to my new discovery of identity and purpose was my relationship with God. I realized that I had chosen many parts of my life but could not choose my purpose. On this journey, all things were created by Him and for Him (Colossians 1:16b).

Journeys are adventurous and not meant to be stagnant. There are good times but also storms and difficult times. Reflecting on life experiences, the most challenging times in my life has further developed my character, faith, and confidence. I also have learned that God accomplishes His work through those who know Him intimately. However, building intimacy is a process and quite necessary for the journey. Patience is needed because it takes years to develop a close relationship. In order for this intimacy to take place and be effective, we must:

- Be willing to set aside time to meet with the Lord daily through prayer.
- Be willing to share everything about ourselves, such as our dreams, goals, friendships, family, finances, and extracurricular activities.
- Become a good listener. The Lord has much to say whether in His word or conviction of the spirit.
- Become attentive. Refrain from being easily distracted with the responsibilities, concerns, and pleasures of life in this world. Our attentiveness in our quiet times with Him brings intimacy.
- Be transparent. Do not hide areas of weakness by trying to exclude this from prayer and conversation with the Lord.
- Be willing to trust. Without trust, there can be no intimacy. Sometimes we distrust because we don't know what God says about Himself and His actions toward us. This is why reading the scriptures is so important. Once His word is firmly anchored in our minds, we will better understand and discover that He is always faithful.

The most profound characteristic of the kind of intimacy that has true merit is a surrendered life (Mark 8:34-35). If you are willing to give yourself fully to the Lord for His use, He will faithfully provide you with a life of peace, comfort, joy, and transforming love that reaches above all understanding.

The journey is designed by God. The decision to take the journey is yours. If you are called into this ministry, you should be wise and make the decision to live a life that brings glory to God rather than yourself. You will be surprised how He will lift you up and bless you abundantly.

Prayer

Dear heavenly Father,

Thank you for calling me to take risk in the midst of my wariness. It does not always feel comfortable when leaving what is safe and familiar. But my faith and trust in You is all I need to accomplish the task that you set before me. Obedience is better than sacrifice. What You will do as a result will change lives forever. For when we walk with You in the light of Your word, what a glory You shed on our way. While we do Your good will, You abide with us still as long as we trust and obey.

In Jesus' name I pray. Amen.

Point to Ponder

'Your journey has molded you for your greater good, and it was exactly what it needed to be. Don't think you've lost time. There is no short-cutting to life. It took each and every situation you have encountered to bring you to the now. And now is right on time' (Asha Tyson).

CHAPTER 2

DEFINING THE MINISTRY AND ITS BOUNDARIES

> *Jesus said,*
> *'The harvest is plentiful but the workers [laborers] are few.'*
>
> *Matthew 9:37*

As defined by *Webster's*, an *entrepreneur* is someone who organizes a business undertaking, assuming the risk for the sake of the profit. My attention was captured by the definition of an *entrepreneurial leader* as described by Richard J. Goossen, director of the Centre for Entrepreneurial Leaders at the School of Business at Trinity Western University. In his published research preface to *Entrepreneurial Leaders: Reflection on Faith at Work, Volume IV*, he writes, 'An entrepreneur is one who sees reality clearly—has a good read on the circumstances; but the entrepreneur is also one who can see possibilities, connections, and the ways in which innovation and creativity can alter that reality.'

In the Bible, the words *servant.* and *minister* are synonyms, and the same are *service* and *ministry*. As a Christian, you are a minister, and when you're serving, you're ministering. However, according to *Webster's Dictionary*, a *minister* is a servant, one authorized to conduct religious service. According to the Bible, a servant is a laborer. For the purpose of this book, we will combine these two definitions into functions.

Entrepreneurial ministry is a partnership of visible testimony that the traditional church can continually be a vital and vibrant avenue for effective ministry without compromise or loss of heritage and sacredness. By leveraging their entrepreneurial gifts, these ministerial Christ followers are compelled to provide community outreach as their vocation or occupation. Many of these ministers are teachers, artists, medical doctors, consultants, counselors, architects, salesmen, etc. who work in their vocation or profession guided by their spiritual gifts of purpose. These spiritual gifts unleash qualities that call for focused prayer, which develops a kingdom culture that nurtures kingdom families in their human and spiritual needs.

In this type of ministry, the world is your territorial boundary. In order to become what you are purposed to be, you must function outside the box and go beyond your normal boundaries to do what you never before dreamed of doing. The ministry will take you where you have never been to obtain your destiny.

Since it is all about kingdom building, entrepreneurial ministry is an unwavering partnership in God's agenda, and its initiatives are destined to reach the masses wherever they are in their hierarchy of social, emotional, economic, and spiritual needs.

Founded on the Principles of Faith

The entrepreneurial ministry is about expanding God's kingdom. It involves living out one's faith in God and utilizing biblical principles in your daily secular work or business. These interactions further lead to sharing Christ with the world as living examples and building Godly families as a result of the labors.

Martin Luther King, Jr., is credited with this quote: 'We are not makers of history; we are made by history.' An entrepreneurial ministry can only be effective and reach its maximum potential by having anointed men and women of God who are led by the spirit of God as leaders. These entrepreneurial ministers operate in faith and prayer, have vision and courage, are continuously guided by biblical principles, and focus on the kingdom. This breed of ministers will become the light that exposes and explores areas of the unknown as they walk by faith to become what God has purposed them to be.

As ministry has become identified with leadership of religious institutions, there has been a tendency to reduce ministry to merely a matter of upholding and spreading the gospel. We must be ever mindful of the wise words of James, the flesh-and-blood brother of Jesus:

> What does it profit, my brethren, if someone says he has faith but does not have works? Can faith save him? If a brother or sister is naked and destitute of daily food, and one of you says to them, 'Depart in peace, be warmed and filled,' but you do not give them the things which are needed for the body, what does it profit? Thus also, faith by itself, if it does not have works, is dead. But someone will say, 'You have faith, and I have works.' Show me your faith without your works, and I will show you my faith by my works. (James 2: 14-18)

Laboring with a Purpose

Historically, laborers are few and, as such, critically needed. The entrepreneurs of faith are called to help fill that need. 1 Timothy 5:17-18 uses the word *ergates* in referring to elders who labor in the harvest, preaching (evangelizing) and teaching (establishing). The *ergates* kind of involvement is described in Matthew 10, where Jesus sent forth the twelve as laborers, and in Luke 10, where He sent forth the seventy as laborers. There are five significant facts that apply to both missions:

1. They were told to 'go'—they went on a brief trip.
2. They were told to 'preach' that the kingdom of God is near.
3. They performed deeds—healed the sick, drove out demons.
4. They were supported by the people to whom they went.
5. They stayed and ministered only where they were welcome.

Today, there are countless opportunities and modalities for meaningful and effective outreach ministry, such as mentoring opportunities, feeding the hungry, prison ministry, ride sharing, teaching literacy, counseling, art therapy, and computer skills training. The effective use of new technologies like websites, blogs, Facebook, and Twitter can also be essential. Social media reaches out across geographical boundaries with positive messages and are effective in building supportive relationships and networks.

Being a minister means making a sacred commitment to spread hope and healing and thereby brings relief to a hurting world. Every time we minister to another person, we are fulfilling Jesus' message that 'the kingdom of God is among you'. Although it is a big responsibility, it is also an incredible honor to be used by God.

Prayer

Dear Father,

Thank you for the awesome task of laboring in order to bring in a harvest. The results will yield meaningful relationships and a kingdom culture.

In Jesus' name, I pray. Amen.

Point to Ponder

'Go where you are celebrated—not tolerated. If they can't see the real value of you, it's time for a new start' (Unknown).

CHAPTER 3

THE STATE OF OUR UNION AND COMMUNITIES

If you learn only methods, you'll be tied to your methods, but if you learn principles you can devise your own methods.

Ralph Waldo Emerson

We all know that flourishing cities often become the means for securing material prosperity. As such, very often in this quest, there is a tendency to forget the Lord. However, the Bible presents the city as a place of God's grace, peace, and prosperity, as well as a place where man secures his own power and prosperity apart from God. The message does present a double standard.

A brief overview of our nation's economy brings to light that for most Americans, things are getting progressively worse. Just over the last decade, middle-class household income has declined by 7 percent. The poverty rate is at a seventeen-year high with 49.7 million Americans living in poverty. Millions are uninsured, and reportedly, one in nine minority kids are uninsured. Our economy is stagnant, good jobs are hard to find, and safety net programs for poor people are quite scarce. In other words, there goes the neighborhood.

Meanwhile, corporations and the wealthy are not paying their fair share of taxes, and the Pentagon has escaped serious budget cuts. Due to our budget deficits, wars, and record-low taxes for corporations and the rich, most of our local communities are in crisis.

The US accounts for nearly half of the world's total military spending. It appears that state and local budgets favor policing and incarceration while schools are underfunded, and young adults face steep college tuition and fewer career choices. This nation continues to fight and occupy abroad when we should be fighting for our true 'homeland security'—thriving local communities. Our basic social services are rationed while military spending is maintained. About 50 percent of the discretionary federal budget supports the most powerful military in history. Although strides are being made by our commander in chief, there is still so much more to be done.

The Multiplicity Multicultural Challenge

Not surprising is the rapid growth of large cities. There is a magnetic function of these cities that draws in people through its production of lifestyles into a world linked by media and cybernetics. Although most of the nation's population lives in cities, the other portion is being urbanized as well.

In the past, it had appeared that most of the world's non-Christians were geographically and culturally distant people in distant places. Our interconnected and multinational cities have caused a shift in frontier missions. The future promotes cross-cultural ministry right here in this nation caused by the greatest migration ever from all hemispheres—south to north, east to west, and from rural to urban.

School Systems

The public schools, as we know, have eliminated every trace of biblical religion from their curriculum. They have adopted a secular—humanist curriculum that leads many children to dishonor their family's religion. The further decline of Christianity in America can be attributed to the public schools that no longer carve out a place for the Word of God, much less His presence. Therefore, students do not feel any type of association.

While it is critical that schools and communities recognize that school violence needs to be addressed, it is also critical that they respect the hopes and rights of the majority of students who are neither perpetrators nor victims of school violence and who want nothing more than to receive a good education in a safe environment.

Most educators and education researchers and practitioners would agree that school violence arises from a myriad of causes and risk factors that include (but not limited to) access to weapons, media violence, cyber abuse, community, bullying, family environments, personal alienation, and more. Basically, our schools are in continuous turmoil and distress.

The Impact of Incarceration on Children

Incarceration is a dynamic process that unfolds over time. To understand the impact of the incarceration process on children, it is necessary to consider separately the short-term effects of the arrest and separation of the child from the parent. The impact of the unavailability of the parent to the child during the period of incarceration and the effects—both positive and negative—of reunion after the incarceration period.

It is also critical to consider whether the child is living with the parent at the time of incarceration, whether a single—or two-parent household is involved, and, in the case of a two-parent household, which parent is incarcerated. Only a small percentage of children live with their fathers as the sole caregiver; it is more usual for children to be living with a single mother prior to incarceration. The most recent figures (Mumola 2000) indicate that 36 percent of state and 16 percent of federal inmate mothers were not living with their children at the time of admission. In contrast, 56 percent of state and 45 percent of federal inmate fathers were not living with their children at the time of their incarceration. Thus, when a parent is incarcerated, it is more likely that children will experience separation from mothers than separation from fathers. Regardless, this has a devastating effect on the security of the child and their self-esteem.

Further Effects of Incarceration

The incarceration rates continue to rise, and so is prison privatization. There are millions of dollars being poured into the prison system, and the private sector reaps huge financial benefits thereof. According to Jamie Fellner of Human Rights Watch, the extraordinary rate of incarceration in the United States wreaks havoc on individuals, families, and communities and saps the strength of the nation as a whole.

According to the International Centre for Prison Studies, the United States has the highest documented incarceration rate in the world (743 per 100,000 population). Russia has the second-highest rate (577 per 100,000), followed by Rwanda (561 per 100,000). Our nation continues to separate families in communities through incarceration.

Churches across America

Although the church may keep the same basic functions, the forms they take must now continually adapt to the pluralized realities of a twenty-four-hour city. Entrepreneurial ministries must connect with the churches that are not equipped to have day and night pastors that serve all cultures, classes, and languages that reside in these existing communities.

The state of our union and community affairs is sorely affected. Entrepreneurial laborers who have vision and are willing to take risk to become change agents are needed. Although change does not often take place overnight for the better, with focused and purposeful prayer, anything is possible. We must be committed for the duration.

Prayer

Dear heavenly Father,

Help us to seek Your guidance before we create new ways of making a difference in our communities and ultimately our society. Help us to identify ways and means to bring needed resources that effect positive change to our communities.

In Jesus' name, we pray. Amen.

Point to Ponder

The future belongs to those who see possibilities before they become obvious. 'For the vision is yet for an appointed time . . . it will surely come, it will not tarry'. (Habakkuk 2:3).

CHAPTER 4

THE MINISTERIAL LIFE OF JESUS CHRIST

> *The Spirit of the Lord is upon me, because he hath anointed me to preach the Gospel to the Poor; He hath sent me to heal the brokenhearted, to preach deliverance to the captives, and recovering of sight to the blind, to set at liberty them that are bruised.*
>
> *Luke 1:18*

C hrist is our supreme example to emulate—whether in our own lives or in ministering to others. As Christians, we are called to be like Christ. Think about the kind of minister Jesus was. Did He do things in his ministry that we can duplicate based on the calling on our life to serve in this ministerial capacity? What this really means is following his example of versatility and nonviolent social change that was at times radical in nature.

Jesus' life exemplified humility. Instead of asserting His divine rights while on earth, He left behind the glory and authority to which He was entitled. Clothed with humanness, Jesus chose to be an obedient servant of His Father (Philippians 2:5-8). We know that the world does not value an attitude or lifestyle of humility; rather it gives accolades to stellar achievement, wealth, genius, and outward beauty. But we are assured by the scriptures that if we choose meekness, living in submission to Jesus as master of our lives, we will be rewarded both in this life and the life to come (Matthew 5:5).

The ministry of Jesus was characterized by the fact that He brought hope and healing into the lives of all He encountered. Jesus was considered versatile and carried His ministry with Him wherever He ventured. However, the places where He ministered were not relevant. At times, He gave eloquent speeches and sometimes simple one-on-one conversations. Whether in a synagogue, campground, alleyway, or a deserted corner, He provided ministry in all these places and then some.

We relate well to the ministry of Jesus based on His and our life experiences. Many of us came from communities and cities that were so downtrodden in every sense of the word that folk could say, 'Can any good thing come from that neighborhood?' Well, we know that Jesus was born into a country that lacked hope for a better future. However, He gave voice to the vision of the world set right and ushered in the reign of a grace filled justice that overcame oppression in all geographical sections of the world. And miraculously, when all hope seemed lost, He proclaimed a greater hope than anything previously imaginable—the hope and joy of salvation. There is no greater gift or love.

Jesus was instrumental in bringing inspiration and hope in people's hearts. He also brought healing to their lives, which He did in tangible ways—feeding the poor, healing the sick, liberating the mentally ill from their demons, forgiving sinners, and teaching them how to forgive and love themselves again. Jesus did not tell people what to believe; He literally showed them the way.

There is no comparison to the personhood of Jesus; however, spoken by the prophet Isaiah, 'He was despised, and we esteemed him not.' Most of the time, Jesus didn't even get addressed respectfully; He was mocked, spat upon, scourged, and nailed to a cross.

Ministry does not mean telling people what they should believe about theological issues. According to the Word, Jesus rarely talked about religious doctrine and left many theological questions unaddressed.

However, despite not having any formal religious education, Jesus impressed teachers in the Jerusalem temple with His intuitive wisdom and understanding. For He was on a mission that was impossible for anyone else to fulfill. He is the true deliverer.

Prayer

Heavenly Father,

Thank You for wisdom, knowledge, and strength. I find joy in sharing Your word as a living example. For You said in Romans 12:1, 'I beseech you therefore, brethren, by the mercies of God, that ye present your bodies a living sacrifice, holy, acceptable unto God, which is your reasonable service.' Show us how we can be more sensitive to the needs of our consumers of service. Help us to hear and to respond quickly and effectively to their areas of need.

In Jesus' name I pray. Amen.

Point to Ponder

> Ministry is identified in many forms and types. It does not necessarily mean being called by a special title that indicates spiritual authority and being worthy of significant respect. Ministry doesn't necessarily mean being the leader of a church. A review of the scriptures reveals that Jesus was never the leader of a synagogue, nor did He hold any priestly or political office. Mostly, His ministry took other forms.

CHAPTER 5

PROBLEM SOLVING IN OUR CURRENT COMMUNITIES

> *The life I touch for good or ill will touch another life and that in turn another, until who knows where the trembling stops or in what far place my touch will be felt.*
>
> *Frederick Buechner (born 1926),*
> *educator, writer, theologian*

There are numerous issues related to the social structure of the community that affect its cohesion and the kinds of interests different groups may wish to protect as they seek solutions to economic and spiritual growth and development. Some of the most salient include ethnicity and language, family structure, cultural issues, and religious divide.

While ethnicity is not necessarily a divisive factor in communities, it certainly can have a divisive effect. It may be compounded by other issues, such as the ways different ethnic groups show respect for authority (God, family structure, and social structure). There must be multiethnic cooperatives and programming for its constituents.

Another potentially divisive factor includes religion and spirituality in communities. In each of these cases, a key question is whether a particular local population's allegiances lie primarily with the community in which it lives or whether it identifies more closely with interests outside the community. A particular religious sect, for example, may be more readily prepared to follow directives of its religious leader than to follow directives from secular leaders within the community. In such cases, community organization for the purpose of governing resources can be difficult. In other cases, however, this is not an issue when all the inhabitants of a community share overriding common interests despite their differences. Sometimes the divisive factors work primarily inside a community. Factions within the community may be organized according to affiliation with a religion, caste, or ethnic group. Even when they do not have strong ties outside the community, these factions can have different interests and concerns that make collective action more difficult.

Family structures often play an important role in creating or limiting social cohesiveness. Many homes are headed by single parents, and the mothers play dual roles due to the absence of fathers. Even though women are working the same jobs as men, on average, they earn less than men and have less opportunity for advancement. Furthermore, confusion over male/female roles and expectations has led to misunderstandings, conflicts, and unstable relationships within parental households.

Adolescents

Due to less supervision and more freedom among children living in various communities of poverty, there is a heightened risk of sexual activity at a younger age.

> Mounting evidence shows that key family and individual characteristics modulate neighborhood effects. At the family level, low socioeconomic status (SES), family disruption, and

residential instability are factors likely to increase exposure to neighborhood peers with more permissive attitudes. For instance, single parents tend to have fewer resources to exert effective supervision than two-parent families and inconsistent supervision is more strongly associated with early sexual activity for adolescents living in disadvantaged neighborhoods. (Dupere 2008)

People's perceptions of resources and their attitudes toward those resources will differ depending on how resources fit into their individual livelihood strategies. Both are trying to look out for their families' economic well-being but with dramatically different effects on the sustainable use of resources.

People's interest in their resource base also varies depending on their level of economic well-being. There is now considerable evidence to suggest that poor people often depend more heavily on governmental systems for sustenance and support. Because of this, they may face very different incentives for their own use of resources, and they may have strong opinions about what the rules for access and exploitation should be. If these concerns are not reflected in the management plans devised by the community, the incentives for some groups *not* to comply with the regulations are likely to be strong.

The success of many community economic efforts depends on people's perceptions that they want to stay in a community and are willing to make investments in it. Conversely, if they expect to leave (or think that their children will do so), their interests may be divergent from those of the rest of the community.

Assessing Community Cohesion

Without partiality to race or class, there are people in every city who seek to repel God's plan for their community. And since our current society gives way to a moral tolerance of unkind deeds, we will continue to entertain immorality, such as greed, injustice, inequality, bigotry, hatred, violence, etc. These types of social behaviors breed at-risk families and communities.

The first issue to assess is whether it is the cohesive factors or the divisive factors in the community that seem to be stronger. In any community, there will be some divisive factors. The question is whether there are also cohesive factors that enable people to overcome their differences in order to engage in collective action.

The community's past experience with collective action is one good indicator of whether people will be able to work together. If people have tried to manage some resource or issue they have in common and have been successful, the incentives to attempt a strategic plan will be stronger than if they had no previous experience or if their previous efforts were unsuccessful. Previous collective action could include anything from yard sales to managing a recreation center. If there has been no attempt to do any of these types of activities, another positive indicator may be a community's ability to organize religious or cultural activities (if all the groups within the community are included).

When an entrepreneurial minister associates with members of the community in the effort to assess through spiritual discernment the tolerable activities that cultivate seeds of hopelessness, it becomes clear that the distasteful results are bred in another realm. When other cultures and ethnicities are present in these same communities and are at odds with each other, this further causes these communities to become strategic objects of attack by enemy forces, making them vulnerable to abuse, division, and ultimately, warfare. The entrepreneurial servant understands the importance of accepting responsibility for the well-being of people in the community. A clear understanding of Jeremiah 29:7 lets us know that cities/communities are prime for evangelism efforts.

What cannot be denied is the fact that on many different social fronts, there are people who are living out their faith, serving God and humanity by serving as advocates for the oppressed, the lost, and the undesirable. As Isaiah 58 explains it, this is true worship and the blessings thereof.

Prayer

Dear heavenly Father,

Thank You for providing me with the ability to understand the importance of community cohesion. I pray that we are able to identify the strongholds that bring down these communities through division and, ultimately, warfare. The entrepreneurial servants will serve as advocates in these times of need for the oppressed, the lost, and those who continue to struggle.

In Jesus' name, I pray. Amen.

Point to Ponder

Vision is the world's most desperate need. There are no hopeless situations, only people who think hopelessly. Where there is no vision, the people perish (Proverbs 29:18).

CHAPTER 6

WORKING FOR GOD IN EXCELLENCE

Everybody can be great. Because anybody can serve. You don't have to have a college degree to serve. You don't have to make your subject and your verb agree to serve . . . . You don't have to know the second theory of thermodynamics in physics to serve. You only need a heart full of grace. A soul generated by love.

Martin Luther King, Jr. (1929-1968), minister, civil rights activist

The most profound message of hope is to imagine a reconciled world in which vast numbers of people of every nation, race, creed, color, and religion gain the hope of a world fully and universally reconciled—a world where we don't hate or hold grudges against one another but rather show mercy and grace. We won't fight with each other over cultural differences or status in society but rather seek peace, understanding, and harmonious coexistence in the knowledge that we are all God's children and that he loves us one and all.

Whatever type of ministry one chooses to do, let us always keep in mind that it is not about raising oneself up above others but about lifting others up through humble service. We are all somebody's reward. We are truly blessed when we can find ways to touch each person in our lives with this magnificent hope. In this type of ministry, we must identify with God and, through His anointing, provide spiritual healing to the souls in our midst and, through prayer, loose the chains of physical suffering and negative thought patterns that may bind them to a distorted view of what is real. Jesus did this and so much more. By this we will know the true meaning of ministry.

Deacon Earnest was one of the first entrepreneurial ministers I ever met. This man was remarkably inspiring because he became an entrepreneur during the early 1960s in the Deep South, when segregation was running wild under Jim Crow laws. He was a self-taught black man with less than a seventh-grade education coupled with limited possibilities. But he was an intelligent man with a heart full of love for the Lord and for humanity that was contagious. God's favor and miracles in his life gave him great confidence. His faith was the glue that marked his life forever and caused him to become a man of influence for many years to come. When I think back about him, he really couldn't have had a regular job for too long because he probably would have been fired for talking about his first love all the time. He was truly an ambassador for Christ.

Although Deacon Earnest had a large family of his own, the size never interfered with his belief that he could provide for their safety and security. However, nothing could stop him from following his call to service and becoming an entrepreneur. It was a calling for him that was bathed in faith. For a man who was locally known as a hard worker and a no-nonsense Christian, this was risky business. But he was burdened with a vision and the dream of establishing a business that would provide for his family and employ and serve others while advancing God's kingdom in the process. He knew he would have to take ownership of this success or failure but was willing to take the risk to find the answers. He shared his vision with his supportive wife, who believed in him as the true head of household and that his spiritual leader was God. Prior to quitting his job as a milk delivery man among other odds-and-ends jobs, he had already purchased his truck and tools to enter the unpopular world of being self-employed. But it was grace and the ministry bursting inside of him and screaming to get out that propelled him forward so that he and others might find hope.

Deacon Earnest served his family and community by creating jobs that were not seasonal, which characterized most of the work in the South at that time. Cotton, soybean, and sugar cane were markets that provided seasonal work, which often left families struggling during the winter months of the year. His paper wood (aka pulpwood) business was open year-round and only affected by precipitation. He was in a position to contract with the local elites, his local neighbors, friends, and others to cut their timber for their income, which ultimately provided income for his business. In addition, he employed family members and locals from the communities. People seeking work came from all walks of life and at times brought their baggage with them. This was when his ministry was in full force. He had to be a leader in the face of opposition and pray that the men show up on time, produce the amount of work according to his strategic plan, do not quit after lunch because the work was too hard or it was too hot to cut wood, etc. He oftentimes counseled and prayed with his employees who had hangovers from the weekend, had spent all their money, and could not go home. Then there were the ones who had families that were cohesive but sickly and no health insurance or money for doctor's visit. He even had a family use his pickup truck every Sunday to take the family to church since he was blessed to have a car, a pickup truck, and his pulpwood truck, which he used strictly for business.

After work during the week and on Saturday mornings, Deacon Earnest and sons delivered cut-up stove wood to customers in the community for their cooking and heating purposes. He continued to serve the community, making friends and spreading the good news of the Lord. He had ups and downs just like the next person, but he believed that God was on his side and never gave up. In the weeks that it rained heavily and he and staff were not able to work in the woods due to the mudslides and flooding, these interim stove wood deliveries made ends meet for his family, and there was always provision.

He became a leading example of walking by faith when everything around him was falling apart. He found the strength and motivation to get up and fight the good fight because he truly believed that he would win, and he did. A street sign which bears his family name in the small town of Marion, Alabama, helps to preserve his memory.

Deacon Earnest was a member of Hopewell Baptist Church for over sixty years. He was the Sunday school treasurer for seventeen years and an active deacon for over fifty years. He was a man of faith, storyteller, great-grandfather, grandfather, and most importantly, he was my father.

Prayer

Dear heavenly Father,

Thank you for the light. For I will let it shine wherever I go. We as a people are transformed by the trouble in our lives. For our light and momentary troubles are essentially achieving for each of us an eternal glory that far outweighs them all.

In Jesus' name, I pray. Amen.

Point to Ponder

'The longer we keep our story in silence, the more powerful it becomes when we speak it' (Dr. Arthur C. Hochberg).

CHAPTER 7

REV. LEON H. SULLIVAN—A MINISTER OF SOCIAL, ECONOMIC, AND CULTURAL CHANGE

> *The hero is one who kindles a great light in the world, who sets up blazing torches in the dark streets of life for men to see by. The saint is the man who walks through the dark paths of the world, himself a light.*
>
> *Felix Adler (1851-1933), intellectual, founder of the Society for Ethical Culture*

I consider myself privileged and blessed to have walked with, learned from, and gained motivation and the belief that I could make a difference in society from an international role model such as Rev. Leon Sullivan.

Immediately after graduating from high school in 1969, I moved to Philadelphia to live with my eldest sister, Thelma Terrence, and family. It allowed me the opportunity to attend college as a commuting student. Her community was newly racially integrated and what I would call stable and well organized during that time. Religion, although different denominations, was strongly practiced in this community. I constantly heard talks about the pastor of Zion Baptist Church, who was turning the city upside down when it came to uplifting impoverished communities that lacked any and everything. From the pulpit, he could clearly see the needs of many Philadelphia communities. This man was Rev. Leon H. Sullivan. He strongly expressed his belief that God has a plan for every city He raises up. He did not ignore the historical axiom 'As the cities go, so goes the nation'.

As a college student and one who had been raised in the church and survived the civil rights movement of the 1960s, I was intrigued by the messages I heard from this man. He preached that thousands were unemployed and yet thousands of jobs were vacant. Reverend Sullivan believed that having jobs was the key to the economic development and true empowerment of African Americans rather than dependence upon public assistance. It was his spirit-filled passion to uplift the underserved in society that propelled him to move forward in the role of an entrepreneurial minister. He walked by faith, took risk, prayed, and believed that through the promises of God, he could make a difference.

Sullivan organized 400 other ministers and launched a 'selective patronage' program whose main purpose was to boycott the Philadelphia-based companies that did not practice equal opportunity in employment. The boycott opened up more than 4,400 jobs to African Americans, yet many still needed to be trained and prepared for those jobs. In response, Reverend Sullivan founded the very first Opportunities Industrialization Center (OIC) in 1964. OIC provided job and life skills training and matched its graduates up with the employment needs of Philadelphia businesses. The undertaking was a huge success, and the programs were replicated in cities across the United States. In 1969, OIC International was created to provide employment-training services on a global scale.

In addition to holding honorary doctorate degrees from over fifty colleges and universities, Reverend Sullivan was awarded the Presidential Medal of Freedom in 1992 by President George H. W. Bush, honoring him for his 'voice of reason for over forty years' and a lifetime of work in helping the economically and socially disadvantaged people in the world.

Reverend Sullivan went on to launch an international campaign to reform apartheid in South Africa, developing the Sullivan Principles, a code of conduct for human rights and equal opportunity for companies operating in South Africa. In the early 1990s, Reverend Sullivan brought world and business leaders together to expand the successful Sullivan Principles into the Global Sullivan Principles of Social Responsibility by developing Bridging the Gaps—the African—African American Summit. The aim of the Global Sullivan Principles was to improve human rights, social justice, and economic fairness in every country throughout the world. Under this pilgrimage, I had the golden opportunity to travel with this powerful leader to Africa twice. And both times, the trip was sponsored by the Philadelphia Department of Commerce, to serve as an ambassador and consultant to the ministers of health on the HIV/AIDS pandemic.

Bridging the Gaps—the African—African American Summit Experience Is Born

It was in the year 1993 that my life went through a metamorphosis. I thank God for role models to emulate. I stepped out on faith and founded Empowerment Resource Associates. Back then, the company's focus was disability management. My main focus was to work with workman's compensation and social security disabilities. I had been well trained in the corporate world to do this, for my title had been disability management consultant for years. However, people with HIV/AIDS started showing up at my office for help. They had no insurance, and some were homeless. During this period the stigma of having HIV/AIDS was devastating. People ran from the thought of associating with someone who had AIDS. Truly, I had not bargained to work with this population either. I wanted to make huge profits from my endeavors. I thought God might have misread my desire to follow His word and direction to serve. At this time, I had a little talk with Jesus and told him all about my troubles with this service. After all, I had to let God know up front that I had no experience working with the HIV/AIDS population. Plus, how was I going to be paid? I was trying to make a living and serve at the same time. After lamenting, I soon remembered that I had seriously given my life to Christ for service; in this case, you don't get to choose your subjects or your geographical boundaries, and you go and serve where you are sent. So I got involved, added this population to my list of clients, and ministered through prevention education and case management to at-risk communities.

By 1995, I decided to certify Empowerment Resource Associates, Inc. as a minority business enterprise (MBE) in order to increase business ventures. When discussing my service programs with the MBE coordinator, only one interest stood out to the Department of Commerce. That was my prevention education work in the area of HIV/AIDS. I was then introduced to the global products and services international trade program and told how major US cities were participants. However, consulting services had never been a part of this trade program. Fortuitously, there was information about Bridging the Gaps—the African—African American Summit taking place within the next six weeks. This summit group was headed to sub-Saharan Africa and led by Rev. Leon H. Sullivan. I was asked to write a proposal for the funding of this one-week expense-paid summit in order that I discuss and promote my prevention education program to a country where lives were being lost by the millions from complications of this virus. It had become a pandemic. After three weeks of waiting to get my sponsorship approved, I now had only three weeks to prepare my family to accept my solo trip of a lifetime. My gift from God! I was a new entrepreneur on my way to Dakar, Senegal, to minister on the topic of HIV/AIDS. I realized I was living out my purpose. I was given an important task to serve in an unfamiliar country, predominately Islamic, whose language I did not understand. I was escorted and provided a translator, who traveled with me during the week when consulting with the ministers of health.

For thou shall go to all that I shall send thee, and whatsoever I command thee thou shalt speak. Be not afraid of their faces: for I am with thee. (Jeremiah 1:7-8)

In addition, I felt honored and protected, for I was traveling on a plane with the Rev. Leon Sullivan, a man of God who prayed several times daily with us for our safety and the effective use of our goods and services that we were bringing to the continent.

Once I returned to America, I immediately founded the Resource Initiatives Giving Hope through Training (RIGHT) Foundation along with my spirited and purpose-driven cofounder, Montee Williams. The mission of this 501(c)(3) organization was to increase awareness and further prevent the spread of HIV/AIDS to at-risk communities through prevention education, support groups, case management, and empowerment counseling. The prevention education programs that were developed at RIGHT are universal. The Philadelphia Department of Commerce sponsored my second summit trip to Accra, Ghana, in 1999 for the same purposes. My work in the RIGHT Foundation proved to me that God had become the pilot of my life. I had clearly given up the notion of making huge financial profits as a living but rather making a living on low pay where the rewards were high on investment in the life of those in need.

What I learned from Reverend Sullivan will stay with me for a lifetime. A man of courage and a servant of the people, Leon H. Sullivan devoted his life to the well-being of others. Reverend Sullivan passed away on 24 April 2001.

Prayer

Lord,

You have said that you will give us new and creative ideas that the Holy Spirit will show us things to come. Father, You know what the community needs are now and what they will be in the future that will bring blessings. Give us fresh ideas and innovative thoughts so that we may develop better goods and services for our cities and communities. These ideas will translate into meaningful relationships that provide spiritual growth and prosperity.

In Jesus' name, I pray. Amen.

Point to Ponder

'The most common way people give up their power is by thinking they don't have any' (Alice Walker).

CHAPTER 8

SOCIAL AND ECONOMIC EMPOWERMENT OF WOMEN

> *We must have a theme, a goal, a purpose in our lives. If you don't know where you're aiming, you don't have a goal. My goal is to live my life in such a way that when I die, someone can say, she cared.*
>
> *Mary Kay Ash (1908-2001), entrepreneur*

Women today are struggling with the balance of attending to the needs of both their families and their careers. Job competition with men, emotional turmoil, less income due to divorce, and single parenthood can wreak havoc on a household.

It was on the spring of 1996 when I met Jayda, a female representative for a local printing company. I had stopped in to get a price quote for new brochures for my empowerment business. Jayda, who appeared to be shy, provided excellent customer service. She was also passionately excited about a new venture she wanted to share with me as I was leaving the store.

It was her kindness in her treatment of my printing that persuaded me to wait and chat with her. Through her passion about the business, she told me that she was a skin care consultant for a huge company. She further went on to say that she planned to leave the printing company in a few months to become a full-time independent contractor for this company. We decided to do lunch one day since my office was in her area.

Jayda's Testimony

As we grabbed a table at an outdoor restaurant, Jayda told me how she was introduced to Mary Kay Cosmetics. She further explained that as she waited for her daughter to finish her piano lesson at the music school, a consultant gave her a card and offered to provide her a free facial at her leisure. Feeling light-headed and nauseated from her earlier chemotherapy treatment, Jayda rudely told the consultant that she did not wear makeup and had no intention of starting. The consultant, also a piano student, was kind, didn't seem offended, and gave her a sample anyway. The next week, they ran into each other again. This consultant seemed to sense that Jayda was ill. She was also empathetic to her and decided to wait with her until Jayda's daughter was finished with her piano lesson. She then gave them a ride home as a simple act of kindness. Being grateful for the ride, a few days later, Jayda called this compassionate woman and requested a facial for herself. As they developed a friendship, she confessed her pain and sorrow to this Christian consultant who ministered to her for weeks before the consultant talked her into becoming a consultant as a way of healing through helping others and building her self-esteem. Jayda went on to explain to me that she was diagnosed with a rare cancer several years ago and given six months to live. Coming from an abused background, at the time age 32, a single parent with a 16-year-old daughter, she was a mess, but she wanted to live. Once she became a consultant, within four months, she was top salesperson in her group. Seventeen months later, she was cancer-free.

After I became one of Jada's customers, she routinely called me to talk about the changes she was making in her life as a result of better friendships and becoming a Christian. Jayda decided to pay if forward and also noticed how she was helping people by listening and supporting them through hardships. The makeup sales business was flourishing but became secondary to her increased self-esteem, as she healed from past hurts while sharing and listening to others.

Meeting the Entrepreneur Who Employed Women Worldwide

I received a flyer from Jayda which advertised that Mary Kay, her employer, was due in Philadelphia to speak at one of the sales conferences. She spoke of how this lady had magically persuaded women to give up welfare—women who were battered and going from shelter to shelter, college students, etc.—and transformed them physically, spiritually, and economically. The lady I am referring to was business leader and entrepreneur Mary Kathlyn Wagner, aka Mary Kay Ash, a pioneer for women in business who built a substantial cosmetics empire. I attended the conference in order to hear this lady's story.

As many of us know, back in the 1960s, the women most crucial to the feminist movement that emerged arrived at their commitment and consciousness in response to the unexpected and often disheartening experience of having their work minimized, and often disregarded, by the men they considered to be their colleagues.

Ash would often express (as she did that evening) how she got started in the business as a precursor in her motivational speech to her audience. She explained that after her bad experiences in the traditional workplace, she set out to create her own business at the age of 45. She started with an initial investment of $5,000 in 1963. She purchased the formulas for skin lotions from the family of a tanner who created the products while he worked on hides. With her son, Richard Rogers, she opened a small store in Dallas and had nine salespeople working for her. Today there are more than 1.6 million salespeople working for Mary Kay Inc. around the world.

The company turned a profit in its first year and sold close to $1 million in products by the end of its second year, driven by Ash's business acumen and philosophy. The basic premise was much like the products she sold earlier in her career. Her cosmetics were sold through at-home parties and other events. But Ash, being a creative entrepreneur, strove to make her business different by employing incentive programs and not having sales territories for her representatives. She believed in the golden rule—treat others as you want to be treated—and operated by the motto 'God first, family second, and career third'. This motto was printed on many of the materials for her distributors. Her approach to business attracted a lot of interest. She was admired for her strategies and the results they achieved.

Ash wanted everyone in the organization to have the opportunity to benefit from their successes. She promoted self-esteem. Sales representatives—Ash called them consultants—bought the products from May Kay at wholesale prices and then sold them at retail price to their customers. They could also earn commissions from new consultants that they had recruited. It multiplied.

She seemed to sincerely value her consultants and once said, 'People are a company's greatest asset.'

She established the Mary Kay Charitable Foundation in 1996. The foundation supports cancer research and efforts to end domestic violence. In 2000, she was named the most outstanding woman in business in the twentieth century by Lifetime Television.

The cosmetics mogul died on 22 November 2001 in Dallas, Texas. By this time, the company she created had become a worldwide enterprise with representatives in more than thirty markets. She will be best remembered for building a profitable business from scratch that created new opportunities for women to achieve financial success, a success that is so needed in our communities for women. This entrepreneurial service business continues to flourish in this twenty-first century.

Prayer

Heavenly Father,

In our workplace we seek workers who have the right gifts and talents for the job. We pray that they have the right character, personality, and the right personal attributes. We ask that they have a spirit and attitude that are pleasing to You, someone who will be an outstanding employee and an excellent coworker, someone who is willing to accept responsibility and take on new challenges and rise to the occasion, someone who is committed and faithful to give his or her best to whatever he or she does. Thank You for sending just the right individual, called and anointed by You to fill the position.

In Jesus' name, I pray. Amen.

Point to Ponder

In this parable, Jesus tells of workers who grumbled that their newly-joined coworkers were being paid the same wage as those who had been laboring for a long while. God is extravagantly generous with all people, and does not hold back any of his grace from those who are new to the faith. (Wages—A Christian perspective from Gospel Ministries.com).

CHAPTER 9

CREATING MODEL COMMUNITIES OF FAITH

> *The ultimate measure of a man is not where he stands in moments of comfort and convenience, but where he stands at times of challenge and controversy.*
>
> *Martin Luther King, Jr. (1929-1968),*
> *minister, civil rights activist*

God is raising up believers all over the world who are experiencing His clear and often dramatic movement in the workforce and other places of influence. Their excellence, integrity, love, and deliberate welcoming of the Holy Spirit's movement are paving the way for Him to use them mightily and bring glory to Himself.

For most entrepreneurs, the goal sought by the corporate leaders throughout history that will continue in the future is profit. We all know that businesses are economic systems designed to use money as the primer of collective action. These professionals are normally trained to focus their corporate attention on the money flow and to maximize return on investment. But the mind of an entrepreneurial minister has a spiritual drive within that threatens to take an equal place with profit as the motivation of executive action. This drive is passed through the business hierarchy and ends up with the rank-and-file workers.

Many Christians like playing it safe by gathering as many facts as possible about a situation. We analyze the options and make choices in order that they are reasonably certain of the outcome. An entrepreneur is known for being a risk taker. In this ministry, one must step out of their comfort zone to do the work that they are called to do. We have a tendency to label risk 'undesirable' because it could end up causing loss and heartache. We fear unwanted results as much as we dread missing out on our dreams. In addition, we fear looking foolish or incompetent, incurring financial difficulty, or facing physical danger. From the human perspective, eliminating uncertainty makes sense. But what is God's perspective? According to the Word, 'Faith without works is dead.' Does this mean that there are times that Christians are to take risks? The answer here is a resounding yes when He is the one asking us to step out of our comfort zone. From the Lord's viewpoint, there is no uncertainty because He has control over all things, and He will never fail to accomplish His good purposes (Ephesians 1:11).

The Bible is full of real people who took risk to obey the Lord. One in particular was Ananias, whom God sent to minister to the newly converted Saul. Ananias risked his reputation and his life to comply. Another was Saul himself, who was told to preach to the Jews the very gospel he and they had so violently opposed. By focusing on God, His character, and His promises, both men obeyed despite uncertainty, doubt, and fear. This is the example of the path of commitment that the entrepreneurial minister must take.

We may have all heard the saying 'It takes a village to raise a child'. In this book, the new phrase is 'Take the city for Christ'. We have been put to the challenge to serve this present age and to be bridge-builders for generations born and unborn.

Biblical scripture gives both negative and positive views of cities. At times, the city exalts the very essence of pride and selfishness (Genesis 4:17-24). However, at other times, the Bible clearly presents the city as a place of refuge (Numbers 35: 6-25), a place of protection (Psalms 48), or a place to secure peace and prosperity (Jeremiah 29:7). For these reasons, Jesus cautioned His disciples to evaluate every city, determining city by city, town by town, who its master is (Luke 10:8-16). There is clearly a direction here for the entrepreneurial ministers to evaluate the needs of these communities, which make up cities, not only for economic and social needs but for their need for the gospel. We must remember that God's primary purpose for the city is not to bring temporal benefits. God intends for these connected communities to be a place of protection and prosperity, ultimately for the reason of drawing people to Himself. In other words, the primary purpose of these communities is to be a tool of evangelism.

In our current society, the fabric of our communities is in shambles. Prayer is not often practiced in our homes and has also been taken out of our schools. While bullies and terrorist are steadily on the rise, law and order significantly violated and diminished, people are hungry, unemployed, and are spiritually, physically, and mentally depleted. Our only hope is to take back our communities through Godly principles and teachings. The sign of the times are here. We must be in the business of winning souls for Christ. We may think our work is irrelevant based on societal changes and a decrease in the support and perceived need for missionaries, but it really has just begun. Children can no longer lead the lives of children even when all the right rules, moral judgment, and values are instilled in them. This fast-paced technological age breeds worldly information into their lives daily, even the lives of infants. There are two dominating schools of thought to act upon: cyber and regular mind manipulation. Clearly, in order to adequately function in society today, you must live by both. We are in spiritual warfare, and as entrepreneurial ministers, we must leverage our spiritual gifts to bring about positive change in all at-risk communities.

Needs of the Community

We learn the needs of the community by communicating directly with people in the community. There is no need to second-guess or be inaccurate about what you think the needs are. Questioning and observation tell the story. For example, the life of Moses certainly reminds us that you don't have to grow up in a community to lead the people there. But knowing some of the indigenous folk can provide some helpful insight. As ministry leaders who care, we must take to the streets and learn the family dynamics of our communities. We must be involved with the basics (e.g. determining who is the head of household, how many live in the home, who goes to school, who goes to work, are there signs of abuse, what kind). Nonetheless, it is often because of ignorance, misperceptions, and fear that the middle class moves out, property values go down, businesses leave, and the ability to help the poor declines. As family and friends see their loved ones trapped in a low standard of living compared to the affluent images of surrounding suburbia, a sense of hopelessness sets in, and the esteem and image of these communities in the city continues on a downward spiral.

> And seek the peace of the city where I have caused you to be
> carried away captive, and pray to the Lord for it; for in its
> peace you will have peace. (Jeremiah 29:7)

Our work in the community is a territorial assignment. God will assist us with our assignment.

> For thou shall go to all that I shall send thee, and whatsoever
> I command thee thou shalt speak. Be not afraid of their faces,
> for I am with thee. (Jeremiah 1:7-8)

Prayer

Dear heavenly Father,

Let us be ever mindful of the needs of our communities. Let us not run away from situations that seem frightful in our communities but begin to seek out and address the issues head-on. Provide us with the wisdom, strength, and knowledge to have hope in the midst of the storms. For You said in Your word that You would never leave or forsake us.

In Jesus' name, I pray. Amen.

Point to Ponder

'Nothing can withstand the power of the human will if it is willing to stake its very existence to the extent of its purpose' (Benjamin Disraeli (1804-1881), prime minister of the United Kingdom).

CHAPTER 10

THE ANOINTED MINISTRY OF MARTIN LUTHER KING, JR.

I am ... The Son of a Baptist Preacher, the Grandson of a Baptist Preacher and the Great Grandson of a Baptist Preacher. The Church is my life and I have given my life to the Church.

Martin Luther King, Jr. (1929-1968),
minister, civil rights activist

Although Coretta Scott (later, King) and I were both born and raised in Marion, Alabama, I was born in the next generation, being four years older than her firstborn, Yolanda King. When attending mass meetings in Marion, Yolanda and I had little to no communication, but I fell in love with her name and decidedly named my daughter Yolanda, (affectionately Yokki) after her. Coretta lived on her father's farm, which was a few miles outside of Marion's city limits where I lived. Her father was an entrepreneur and farmer. According to the Little Known Black History Facts, Mr. Obadiah Scott was the first African American to own a pulpwood truck in the county. He and my dad had a lot in common, for they were competitors in the pulpwood business.

Living in Marion, Alabama, during my teenage years brought radical excitement. There was a distinguished man (Ms. Coretta's husband) who often drove past our home to visit his in-laws along with his wife and children. Whenever he appeared in town, we all knew there was going to be a town meeting that involved all the local communities from far and near. Community organizers would already have the agenda set before our mass meetings began, which took place at least twice in one week. This inspiring man was Martin Luther King, Jr., a Baptist minister, activist, and prominent leader in the African American civil rights movement. His nonviolent leadership had been discussed in our home and at the Marion Baptist Academy (my school from kindergarten through tenth grade) all too often. When Dr. King would preach on how we were made in the image of God and His likeness, should love our neighbor as ourselves, and that we were created equal, he planted seeds of hope and love in my heart that I had not experienced before. One thing for sure, I saw people in those mass meetings that I had never seen before at anybody's church, and my family visited many. I believed that most of the people were there because they heard that someone cared about their needs. They were especially captivated by the genuine care and concern from this preacher and entrepreneurial minister who walked among them.

My mother was a housewife who owned a car. She was committed to the civil rights movement and felt it was her duty to provide transportation for friends and neighbors who needed a ride to the mass meetings. I remember how efficiently she had dinner ready on the dates of the meetings in order that Dad would not feel slighted when she needed to leave an hour early to make her pick-up rounds. When she told a couple of her friends that two local cab drivers had stopped speaking to her, they laughed and told her that the cab drivers had threatened to report her to authorities for blocking their business and running an underground taxi service. She was furious about the accusation but soon realized that the cab drivers thought she was receiving a fare when all she required from her passengers was friendly conversation and occasional gas money when gas was low, which they collected among themselves as a token of appreciation.

News headlines of boycotts, authorized and unauthorized nonviolent marches, riots, beatings and bombing, and civil unrest plagued the linking cities of Marion—Selma, Montgomery, and Birmingham, Alabama—where many of my family members lived. As a young teenager, I was traumatized by many of these events, especially the march over the Edmund Pettus Bridge (Bloody Sunday site). The happenings from that event left an indelible mark on my life. However, it was events such as this that made me aware, angry, resilient, and more determined to fight for justice in our communities than ever despite the cost.

Integration for Marion, Alabama

It was our nonviolent marches for social change that had a major influence in having the desegregation laws put in place. Changes were taking place all over the state of Alabama under the leadership of Dr. King, who made it clear that the civil rights cause was based on his belief in God, although he was alleged to have been connected to the Communist Party, which is based on atheistic philosophy rejecting religion.

It was 1967, the year that Marion Baptist Academy was dissolved due to desegregation laws. There were only two private schools in town at the time: Perry Christian School (white) and Marion Baptist Academy (black). In order to remain open, they both would have to integrate in order to receive their single grant from the state that covered transportation, books, and other educational material, which was crucial during that time. Since neither school would concede, both closed their doors for good in June 1967. As a direct result, I graduated from a public school, Francis Marion High, the first integrated high school in Marion, Alabama, in 1969.

Like many in the Bible who were persecuted for their ministry, King further established his reputation as a radical and became an object of the FBI's COINTELPRO for the rest of his life. But being led by the Holy Spirit, King moved in obedience to the Word of God. Little did we know that this man would one day receive the Nobel Peace Prize for combating racial inequality through nonviolence. He was truly the humanitarian in every sense of the word. However, his efforts were successfully bathed in the Word of God. In the next few years leading up to his death, he expanded his focus to include poverty and the Vietnam War, alienating many of his liberal allies with a 1967 speech entitled 'Beyond Vietnam'. King was planning a national occupation of Washington, DC, called the Poor People's Campaign.

King was assassinated on 4 April 1968 in Memphis, Tennessee. He was posthumously awarded the Presidential Medal of Freedom in 1977 and Congressional Gold Medal in 2004; Martin Luther King, Jr., Day was established as a US federal holiday in 1986. Hundreds of streets in the US and beyond have been renamed in his honor.

Prayer

Dear heavenly Father,

Thank You for the courage and the faith to stand up for what one believes in his heart to be right no matter the cost. Lord, help us to be the most valuable servants possible, ones who are sensitive to the needs of others as we perform our duties. Thank You, Father, for the creativity that is evident in the different areas of our work. Continue to fill us with new ideas and new service concepts.

In Jesus' name, I pray. Amen

Point to Ponder

'Let every man abide in the same calling wherein he was called' (1 Corinthians 7:20).

CHAPTER 11

SERVICE AND SIGNIFICANCE

God has given each of you some special abilities; be sure to use them to help each other, passing on to others God's many kinds of blessings.

1 Peter 4:10

Service is the pathway to significance. It is going to be through ministry that we discover the meaning of our lives. Your heart represents the source of all your motivations toward being a change agent in the community. It involves what you love to do and what you care about most. Your heart reveals the real you and who you truly are, not what others think you are or what circumstances force you to be. The projects you take on as an entrepreneurial minister are the ones that you feel passionate about. The nature of your heart will be revealed by what captures your attention. How do you know when you are doing ministry from the heart? The first sign will be enthusiasm. When you are doing your love or your interest, no one has to motivate, challenge, or check up on you. You are on it wholeheartedly.

Although the needs of the community determine your priorities, your motivation to do this work is not primarily need based. When we become need driven, our priorities change, and we get caught up into funding of same. Most of all, the ministers get burned out over the years. We need to look at the social and spiritual aspects of the neighborhoods. Aesthetically, we know that communities can be run-down and unsightly. The systems do not work. However, families need to become healthy and thrive in a healthy environment. Therefore, the persons in the community need to be spiritually transformed in order to socially transform the places in which they live.

Many children, who seek behavioral health service just because they were referred, do not believe they will live to be 25 years old. They have accepted gun violence, physical, emotional, and sexual abuse as the norm. Some days their spirits are better than others, but basically, they believe their lives will never amount to anything. How do you change that mentality? Sometimes, maybe one child at a time through the following:

- Spend some quality time with them that will ultimately keep them off the streets, and keep them focused on positive activities.
- Develop innovative programs utilizing the thought contributions from adolescents by holding focus groups.
- Motivate them into action by developing their own ideas. Reward them for a job well done.
- Let your light shine before them such that the contagion of your actions multiply your following. Most importantly, discuss with them where your light comes from.
- Tell them your personal testimony and how you came to love what you do and share it with them.
- Teach them how to hold a conversation with God and trust that He hears them. Some of these seeds of knowledge will fall on fertile ground.

When it comes to leadership in these communities, you don't have to grow up there to lead and understand the people, but you do need some indigenous folk on your team.

Prayer

Dear heavenly Father,

Thank You for creating us to add to life on earth, not just take from it. We know that You redeemed us to do Your holy work. For we are not saved by our service but to do service. Help us to act on the things that we know and practice what we claim to believe.

In Jesus' name, we pray. Amen.

Point to Ponder

'Challenges are what make life interesting and overcoming them is what makes life meaningful' (**Joshua J. Marine**).

CHAPTER 12

DETERMINING YOUR CALL TO THE ENTREPRENEUR'S OUTREACH MINISTRY

> *The only way to do great work is to love what you do. If you haven't found it yet, keep looking. Don't settle.*
>
> *Steve Jobs*

For most entrepreneurs, the goal sought by the corporate leader throughout history is profit. The goal of profit will continue in the future. We all know that businesses are economic systems designed to use money as the primer of collective action. These professionals are normally trained to focus corporate attention on the flow of money and to maximize return on investment.

However the mind of an entrepreneurial minister has a drive within that threatens to take an equal place with profit as the motivation of executive action. This drive is passed not only through the business hierarchy but through the rank-and-file workers. This drive is a gentle spirit with a Midas touch that empowers the individual it comes in contact with. Once you are clear that there is a calling in your life, remain dependent on the Holy Spirit for direction.

However, as it is written: 'No eye has seen, no ear has heard, no mind has conceived what God has prepared for those who love him'—but God hath revealed them unto us by his Spirit. The Spirit searches all things, even the deep things of God. (1 Corinthians 2: 9-10)

Another important point is to know your inner spirit, for God has not given us a spirit of fear but one of love and understanding. Their sense of spiritual wholeness defines human action through these guided principles and values. Spirituality to this leader is the capsule that puts the action into play. Their individual sense of who they are as spiritual leaders defines them. Leaders are destined to get in touch with their own spiritual values.

The entrepreneurial minister operates in uniqueness of character. You will know them by their exemplary qualities as believers. There are six key qualities you will see exhibited by these ministers.

1. **Excellence as the currency and authority**

    God, whose spirit is operating in them, is highly regarded as their CEO. Therefore, excellence is the currency and authority in the workplace. Before many people will trust and listen to you, they must first respect you. The entrepreneur's work is done 'unto the Lord' (Colossians 3:23) and will stand apart because of it. Doing an inferior job is not even a concept in the workplace. However, doing a superior job will provide the opportunity to present Christ in a positive light much easier than doing work of poor quality and making an excuse for it. A job well done will always have merit. Have you heard of the saying 'People don't care what you know until they know that you care'? When you genuinely take an interest in another person, whether in your workplace or surrounding community, your witness develops authentic credibility. Your love is felt by others, and you will stand out from the crowd.

2. Ethics

Ethics to the entrepreneurial minister is more than just a set of rights and wrongs. It's embracing the way of Jesus as one tackles the significant challenges of the day—and hoping to find connection in this work. In business, all ethics are determined and displayed by the leadership. The leaders of an organization or company must be determined to follow a personal and business code of ethics. People learn from these examples, not from what they are told to do. The importance of ethics in business is that it sets the tone for a business's success or failure.

3. Integrity

Integrity is the key component to a good life. Our purpose, destiny, and well-being depend on it. Openness to love and intimacy, the ability to stay close to God—all are determined by how well we follow our hearts.

With integrity, we live; without it, we die. Being untrue to your heart is destructive. But if you follow your heart, it will create heaven on earth for you. Each choice in life is a fork in the road. Which one will you take? Where will you end up? It depends on how well you obey your heart. Psalm 51:6 says that God 'desires truth in the inward parts'. Integrity basically means whatever you are in the public eye; you are the same behind closed doors.

4. Humility

As one of God's chosen people, holy and dearly loved, the entrepreneurial minister must be clothed with compassion, kindness, humility, gentleness, and patience. They are inclined to have wisdom, understanding, and insight. Humility is an essential attitude for success in the spiritual life. Any self-conceit—whether nurtured by superior intelligence, wealth, a high position, or the praise of others—is an obstacle on the path.

Leaders who want to grow signal to followers that learning, growth, mistakes, uncertainty, and false starts are normal and expected in the workplace; and this produces followers and entire organizations that constantly keep growing and improving. A sense of humility is essential to leadership because it authenticates a person's humanity. You either genuinely want to grow and develop or you don't, and followers pick up on this.

According to Mike Myatt, chief strategy officer of N2growth, humility is actually the trait that magnifies all other positive attributes. Without humility, all of a leader's other strengths become diminished, if not invisible. It's been said that greatness lies not in trying to be somebody but in trying to help somebody. Humility also happens to be the surest sign of authenticity in someone who claims to be a servant leader. Is it possible to be a leader without being humble? Sure it is. But it is much more difficult, rarely sustainable, and leaders who lack humility are always called into question with regard to motives and agendas.

When you think of a true leader, do you envision someone who displays a quiet confidence or a blatant arrogance? A reserved attitude of humility can often be misinterpreted as a sign of weakness. However, if you've negotiated with a truly confident person who is authentically humble, you'll find that their resolve is often much greater than the feigned confidence of the arrogant. It was C. S. Lewis who said, 'Humility is not thinking less of yourself, but rather thinking about yourself less.' Simply put, humble leaders recognize and value the contributions of others in lieu of self-promotion.

5. Prayer power—a catalyst for supernatural change

One of the attributes of an effective witness is a move of the Holy Spirit through focused prayer. The entrepreneurial minister must pray for the organization singly and corporately and must equip workplace employees by welcoming the move of the Holy Spirit in our places of employment. One must remain focused forward, forget what lies behind, and reach forward to what lies ahead (Philippians 3:13). Those weighed down with problems from the past lose sight of the goal. Prayer is a mighty force for the children of God. It pulls down strongholds and clears the path for growth and maturity in those to whom it is directed.

6. Operate in confidence and commitment

As the Word says, 'Trust in the Lord with all your heart, your mind, and soul, in all your ways acknowledge him and he will direct your path.'

The entrepreneurial minister is likely to stumble when we doubt our ability to do what God requires. However, when that confidence is placed in the Lord instead of in oneself, they can move ahead, knowing that He'll enable them to do His will. We know that the Lord promises to guide us as we run the race, provide whatever is needed, and strengthen us along the way. However, one must be committed to Him and determined to carry out His will.

Prayer

Dear Father,

We will follow Your word and obey your commands. We will keep your words at the center of our hearts. For they are life, healing, and health to our souls. Father, our delight and desire are in Your law, and on it we habitually meditate. Thank You for blessing us and keeping us.

In Jesus' name, I pray. Amen.

Point to Ponder

In the Matthew chapter 13 parable, Jesus uses the metaphor of a sower spreading seeds as a way of illustrating that people respond in different ways to the message of the gospel. Some hear and take it to heart; others reject it. But the sower continues to make the message available to all.

CHAPTER 13

THE POWER OF FOCUSED PRAYER

> *Prayer is an invisible tool which is wielded in a visible world. For the weapons of our warfare are not carnal, but mighty through God to the pulling down of strong holds.*
>
> *2 Corinthians 10:4*

Just as there are different types and styles of prayers, there are different ways of praying. Contrary to what we may think, there are no strict rules which need to be followed. However, there are biblical guidelines that can be utilized. The important point to remember in prayer is to pray from the heart. Since God is the recipient of your prayers, He is truly the one who ultimately knows your sincerity and innermost desires.

One of the greatest needs in the Christian community is for Christians to discover and experience the privilege and power of effective prayer. Dr. Bill Bright writes, 'History records no significant movement of the Spirit of God that has not been preceded by a very strong prayer emphasis. And understandably so, because the omnipotent God has chosen to communicate with individuals through prayer as well as through His inspired Word.'

Seriously speaking, if you don't pray often, you won't gain a love for praying. Because prayer is work, it is not very appealing to our natural sensibilities. But the rule for prayer is simple: if you begin a prayer life, your taste for prayer will increase. The more you pray, the more you will acquire the desire for prayer. As you become energized by regular prayer, your sense of purpose in prayer will be illuminated.

Instead of using prayer exclusively to focus on ourselves and present our needs to the Lord, we should see it as a time to let Him fill us with a greater sense of who He is and further develop a sense of why our confidence in Him should never be misplaced. Prayer should begin in our homes. It is the essential ingredient that holds families together.

> The great people of the earth today are the people who pray! I do not mean those who talk about prayer; or those who say they believe in prayer; or those who explain prayer; but I mean those who actually take the time to pray. They have not time. It must be taken from something else. *That something else is important, very important and pressing, but still, less important and pressing than prayer.* There are people who put prayer first, and group the other items in life's schedule around and after prayer. These are the people today who are doing the most for God in winning souls, in solving problems, in awakening churches, in supplying both men and money for mission posts, in keeping fresh and strong their lives far off in sacrificial service on the foreign field, where the thickest fighting is going on, and in keeping the old earth sweet a little while longer. (S. D. Gordon, emphasis added)

Up in a little town in Maine, things were pretty dead some years ago. The churches were not accomplishing anything. There were a few Godly men in the churches, and they said: 'Here we are, only uneducated laymen; but something must be done in this town. Let us form a praying band. We will all center our prayers on one man. Who shall it be?' They picked out one of the hardest men in town, a hopeless drunkard, and centered all their prayers upon him. In a week, he was converted. They centered their prayers upon the next hardest man in town, and soon he was converted. Then they took up another and another, until within a year, two or three hundred were brought to God, and the fire spread out into all the surrounding country. Definite prayer for those in the prison house of sin is the need of the hour. (Dr. R. A. Torrey)

Spurgeon's boiler room. Five young college students were spending a Sunday in London, so they went to hear the famed C. H. Spurgeon preach. While waiting for the doors to open, the students were greeted by a man who asked, 'Gentlemen, let me show you around. Would you like to see the heating plant of this church?' They were not particularly interested, for it was a hot day in July. But they didn't want to offend the stranger, so they consented. The young men were taken down a stairway, a door was quietly opened, and their guide whispered, 'This is our heating plant.' Surprised, the students saw 700 people bowed in prayer, seeking a blessing on the service that was soon to begin in the auditorium above. Softly closing the door, the gentleman then introduced himself. It was none other than Charles Spurgeon.

> Eighteen-year-old Hudson Taylor wandered into his father's library and read a gospel tract. He couldn't shake off its message. Finally, falling to his knees, he accepted Christ as his Savior. Later, his mother, who had been away, returned home. When Hudson told her the good news, she said, 'I already know. Ten days ago, the very date on which you tell me you read that tract, I spent the entire afternoon in prayer for you until the Lord assured me that my wayward son had been brought into the fold.' (*Our Daily Bread*, 19 July 1989)

Hudson Taylor (1832-1905) was a famous missionary in China. He was founder of the China Inland Mission which, at his death, included 205 mission stations with over 800 missionaries and 125,000 Chinese Christians. He spent fifty-one years in China.

> Men and women are needed whose prayers will give to the world the utmost power of God; who will make His promises to blossom with rich and full results. God is waiting to hear us and challenges us to bring Him to do this thing by our praying. He is asking us, to-day, as He did His ancient Israel, to prove Him now herewith. Behind God's Word is God Himself and we read: 'Thus saith the Lord, the Holy One of Israel, and his Maker: Ask of me of things to come and concerning my sons, and concerning the work of my hands, command ye me.' As though God places Himself in the hands and at the disposal of His people. Without such faith it is impossible to please God, and equally impossible to pray. (E. M. Bounds, *Weapon of Prayer*)

Prayer

Dear heavenly Father,

We know that our prayer power has never been tried to its full capacity. If we want to see mighty wonders of Your divine power and grace wrought in the place of weakness, failure, and disappointment, we must respond to Your standing challenge, 'Pray without ceasing'.

In Jesus' name, I pray. Amen.

Point to Ponder

'The man who mobilizes the Christian church to pray will make the greatest contribution to world evangelization in history' (Andrew Murray).

CHAPTER 14

AMBASSADORS FOR CHRISTIAN COMMUNITY DEVELOPMENT

Saint Paul said that 'God was reconciling the world to himself in Christ, not counting people's sins against them. God reconciled us to himself through Christ and gave us the ministry of reconciliation: As such, we are therefore Christ's ambassadors, as though God were making his appeal through us.

2 Corinthians 5:18-20

The world moves more quickly than ever, with no signs of slowing down. As we ride this roller coaster of life, we have accepted a 'faster is better' mindset, which has created a culture that allows us to look at, rather than see, what's around us. Our communities remain in turmoil. However, unless a community changes from the inside out, there has not been a visit from God. The catalyst to this change will be the focused prayers of Christians who truly believe yokes can be broken and strongholds that imprison its people torn down. The entrepreneurial ministry is an outreach extension of the church. It does not in any way take the place of the church. However, it is a partnership between the urban and suburban church and between business people who are inclined toward revitalization and revival.

The spiritually attuned entrepreneurs accept as their prime goal the need to help their consumers of service become their best self as the business itself strives to maximize profit for the well-being of all involved. This is a daunting task. God determines your greatness by how many people you serve, not how many people serve you.

In Matthew 25, Jesus shares a vision of heaven and the King of Glory sitting on His eternal throne. At the judgment, the risen Christ will say to His righteous ones, 'For I was hungry and you gave Me food; I was thirsty and you gave Me drink. I was a stranger and you took Me in: I was naked and you clothed Me. I was sick and you visited Me, I was in prison and you came to visit Me' (35-36).

These ambassadors are on the lookout for ways to help others. They make themselves available. They do not make excuses, procrastinate, or wait for better circumstances to take place. At times, working in the trenches is the only option. You will never arrive at the stage in life where you are too important to help with menial task. For these tasks are parts of your character curriculum. Jesus specialized in menial task that everyone else tried to avoid, such as washing feet, feeding the hungry, and helping the needy. Nothing was beneath Him because He was true to His mission: He came to serve. Remember, doing small tasks often show a big heart. Your servant's heart is revealed in small acts that others won't think of doing. That ultimately results in big opportunities that are often disguised.

If you are currently serving in obscurity in some small place, feeling unappreciated, God has you there for a purpose. Stay put until He chooses to move you. God is aware of everything that involves you. He will surely let you know if He wants you somewhere else.

Your mission is a wonderful privilege, and although the entrepreneurial ministry is a big responsibility, it is also an incredible honor to be used by God. As His ambassador or representative, we get to partner with God in the building of His kingdom. God uses us to persuade men and women to drop their differences and enter into His work of making things right between them. We become the speakers for Christ Himself as we perform our daily duties.

Your mission will impact the eternal destiny of other people. The consequences of your community ministry will last forever. Nothing else you do will ever matter as much as helping people establish an eternal relationship with God. These are such exciting days to be alive. Most of the world now thinks globally. The largest media and business conglomerates are all multinational. Our lives and work is increasingly intertwined with those in other nations as we share everything from products and services to spirituality. The Great Commission is your commission. The secret to living a life of significance is doing your part in the process.

Prayer

Father,

I realize that before I can love others as You have instructed me, I must love myself. Help me to speak with integrity, deal with integrity, and live in harmony with You, myself, and others. I am Your workmanship, recreated in Christ Jesus that I may do those good works which You predestined for me to do. You are my confidence.

In Jesus' name, I pray. Amen.

Point to Ponder

'Conscience is the root of all true courage; if a man would be brave let him obey his conscience' (James Freeman Clarke (1810-1888), preacher and author).

QUOTATIONS

I acknowledge and thank the following people for the quotes used in this book.

REFERENCES

All biblical references are from the King James Version of the Bible.

Ash, Mary Kay Foundation: Mary Kay Ash. (2013). *The Biography Channel website.* <http://www.biography.com/people/mary-kay-ash-197044>.

Dupere, David Paul, Psy.D., Psychologist, Family Life Counseling Service.

Fellner, Jamie; Human Rights Watch Publication, 2006.

Goossen, Richard J., *Entrepreneurial Leaders: Reflections on Faith at Work* (Vol. 4). Langley, BC: School of Business, Trinity Western University, 2008.

Jacobson, Stephen. Spirituality and Transformational Leadership in Secular Settings: A Delphi Study (an abridgement of an unpublished dissertation completed in 1994).

King, Jr., Martin Luther Foundation: Martin Luther King Jr. (2013). *The Biography Channel website.* <http://www.biography.com/people/martin-luther-king-jr-9365086>.

Mumola, C. J. *Incarcerated parents and their children.* Washington, DC: US Department of Justice. (2000).

Myatt, Mike, Chief Strategy Officer, N2growth, Leadership Matters—The CEO Survival Manual.

Our Daily Bread Publication, 19 July 1989.

Sullivan, Leon H. Foundation: Excerpts at <http://www.thesullivanfoundation.org>.

Woodward, George, Ink and Spirit: Literature and Spirituality, 1994.

ABOUT THE AUTHOR

Judy Benjamin Henderson is the founder and CEO of Empowerment Resource Associates Inc., a community-based outpatient mental-wellness and behavioral health clinic. She is also the founder of the Resource Initiatives Giving Hope through Training (RIGHT) Foundation, a community-based 501(c)(3) social service agency dedicated to preventing the spread of HIV/AIDS and other chronic degenerative diseases, namely hypertension and diabetes, through education.

She completed her undergraduate studies in business administration at La Salle College, a master of human services degree from Lincoln University, a master of science degree in organizational dynamics from the University of Pennsylvania, and a post-master's certificate in couples and family therapy from Drexel University.

Judy was recently named Woman of the Year by the National Association of Professional Women. She is the co-chair of the mentoring and networking committee of Chester County Alumni Chapter of Lincoln University. Her Philadelphia offices and suburban Chester County offices serve as community education sites for practicum, volunteer, and work-study students from Lincoln University, Drexel University, Philadelphia College of Osteopathic Medicine, and the University of Pennsylvania.

A trainer and international public speaker, Judy is known for conducting training assignments with the US Postal Service, the Greater Philadelphia Chamber of Commerce, the National Minority AIDS Council, the Balm in Gilead, and the University of Mississippi, just to name a few. She has provided ministry consultations, working closely with the ministers of health in three African countries, namely Ghana, Senegal, and Nigeria.

Judy is the author of *The Empowerment Link Project*, a faith-based crisis intervention partnership program for community behavioral health. She has written articles for the *Continue Care Coordinator* magazine and a health-care industry newsletter, *The Proclamation*.

An active member of St. Paul's Baptist Church in West Chester, Pennsylvania, Judy has served as chairwoman of Women's Fellowship, consultant for the Ministry of Christian Compassion, and active participant of the visitors' ministry. She is a founding member of Playback Theater for Community Social Change, an improvisational drama team designed to bring community peace and reconciliation.

Judy is the wife of Robert A. Henderson, Sr. They reside in rural Chester County, Pennsylvania.